Truth Seekers Kids Magazine

June - 2022 | Issue 9
**TS Kids Magazine Team**

**Mentor**
Maulana Syed Abul Qasim Rizvi
& Syed H. Riza

**Contributors**
Jafar Hasan, Rabab,
Zahra Hasan, Smana Ali

**Designer/Artwork**
TS Kids Creative Team

**Graphics/Images**
TS Kids Creative Team,
Zeeshan Rizvi

For subscription, advertising,
feedback and correspondence
please contact:

**magazine@tskids.club**

 **TSKidsClub**   **TSKidsClub**

# From the
# Editor's Desk

Dear Readers,

Salam un Alaykum,

With the grace of Allah (swt), we are pleased to publish Issue 9 of the TS Kids Magazine.

In this issue, we start with the story of our teenage superhero Muhammad who travels from Canada to Pakistan with his family. At the airport, he finds himself in the middle of some trouble. Read the superhero story to find out more. Without giving spoilers, there is a surprise visit by another superhero at the end! In the Lessons with Grandpa story, wise Grandpa teaches us about Taqwa (God-consciousness) during fasting. Moving along we have Al-Kisa's Animals in the Quran series as a comic with the story of Prophet Musa (peace be upon him). Then we have excellent articles on the battle of Ohad (following the battle of Badr in the previous issue) and Ancestors of Prophet Muhammad (peace be upon him). We also share some wisdom with Mathematica and the Nahjul Balagha series. As usual you will find activities such as Cryptogram, Arabictivity, puzzles and much more which will surely keep you busy and enlightened. From this issue onwards, we will also introduce real-life local superheroes who have greatly contributed to our community.

As you may be aware, we have recently launched the Truth Seekers Members Hub. Look inside for details on how to become a member. We have recently self-published some excellent picture-books for young readers including a series of 4 short books - Know Your Faith. They are freely available if you are a TS Member and you may also buy them from our website. We have also successfully published the 2nd issue of TS Illumination magazine for adults. Make sure to order a copy of TS Illumination if you are not a TS member yet.

We sincerely appreciate and rely on your continued support and prayers.

JazakAllah khair.

TS Editorial Team

# The Helper

By Jafar Hasan

This verse is so beautiful... "but sufficient is your Lord as a Guide and Helper." (Quran 25:31)
Yes, indeed. The names of Allah, Al-Haadi and An-Naseer, surely belong to Allah alone. Only He guides and helps everyone.
By the way, we are about to land now. Make sure you don't roam around at the airport or you might get lost my dear.

Ugh! Luggage always takes a long time to come. I need to go to the toilet. I will come back soon.
I'll quickly charge my iPad and convert some currency too.
Okay Muhammad just go to the toilet and come back soon. We will wait here.

Oh no, how far have I walked?! No charging station is available. I should at least find a place to convert my dollars to rupees.

Oh really! But I am supposed to go back to my parents soon. I also need to quickly charge my iPad. Do you know any place where I can charge it, so I can text my dad?
Hey there! I know a dollar exchange place, where you can get very good rates. It is just 5 minutes from the airport. I can take you there and bring you back, if you want.
Foreign Exchange

Thank you so much.
Yes, sure. You can charge your iPad in the currency shop and inform your parents. The shop owner is my friend.

On my motorbike, don't worry. We will return in no time. I help many people like this.
Is it far? How will we go?

Your iPad appears to be one of the latest models. How many dollars have you got? What else do you have in your bag?
Nothing in my bag. Can you please take me back to the airport? I don't need dollar conversion.
I made this decision in a rush. What have I done? My parents must be waiting for me. I need to get out of here in any way... Oh Allah, you are the true Guide (Al-Haadi) and Helper (An-Naseer). Please help me!

Superhero Abdullah arrives
We are here now. Just two minutes and we are done.
Do you need some help buddy?
TO BE CONTINUED...
Get the next issue to find how our two superheroes, Muhammad and Abdullah, tackle the thug

# Grandpa on God-consciousness

*By Rabab*

"Ohh I am so thirsty and tired", Yusuf complained as he flung his bag to a corner and lied on the couch as if all his energy had drained out. "Today is a very hot day, I feel thirsty too!", added Jamila as she too entered the living room carrying her school bag.

It was the Holy month of Ramzan and like everyone else in the house, Yusuf and Jamila were also fasting to reap the benefits of holy month of Ramzan. Grandpa, who was sitting in the living room reading his Quran looked at the two apples of his eyes and smiled. "Assalamo alykum my precious gems, how was your day at the school?", Grandpa asked. Yusuf still lying on the

couch, replied quickly "Walaikum salam Grandpa, it was so hot and tiring today, I think I can't take it anymore without drinking water. I wish I was an angel, and I didn't have to fast". Grandpa chuckled at Yusuf's wish and looked towards Jamila "Do you wish the same my lovely granddaughter?", he asked her curiously.

Jamila pondered for a while and replied carefully "No Grandpa, I don't wish to be an angel because humans are greater than angels, aren't they?". "Yes, that is correct my dear, but we don't have this status by birth. We can be higher than the angels only if we follow the path of righteousness as laid upon by Islam".

"Yes, that is true Grandpa, and that is why I am fasting every day in the holy month of Ramzan", Jamila said with excitement in her voice.

"But sometimes fasting is really difficult Grandpa, especially when we have school on hot days. I lose all my hydration and energy, I can barely move a limb", Yusuf complained. Jamila who was getting concerned about her little brother said "You don't have to fast Yusuf, you are not baligh yet, you are still too young".

"But everyone in the house fasts, I wanted to try too!", Yusuf replied with a weak voice.

Grandpa stood up from his prayer mat, folded it neatly, and sat next to Yusuf on the couch. He was holding the Holy Quran in his hands. He bent towards Yusuf, politely kissed him on the forehead and said, "My little boy, let me tell you the secret of fasting".

"Secret?, does fasting also has a secret Grandpa?" he questioned surprisingly. "Yes my child, every act of worship for Allah has a secret". Grandpa replied.

"Oh I want to know the secret of fasting too", Jamila cried and excitedly sat next to Grandpa on the couch. Yusuf who was lying until now was curious to know the secret of fasting. He sat up straight and both kids were looking keenly at Grandpa.

Grandpa started "Yusuf, what makes angels different from us?". "Angels don't eat, drink or sleep. They are always obedient to Allah and worship him sincerely", Yusuf replied with confidence. "That's correct! whereas humans need to eat, drink and sleep to stay alive. But Allah, our Lord makes us fast for an entire month. During fasting we do not eat or drink. We obey the commands of Allah, we remember Him and worship Him. So now what is the difference between the person who is fasting and an angel?", Grandpa asked the kids.

"Oh, I see Grandpa, a fasting person is very similar to an angel!" Jamila quickly replied, following Grandpa's line of thinking.

"Yes, but being a human, our need and desire towards food and drink doesn't subside. We still become thirsty and hungry but to obey Our Lord, we bear the thirst and hunger patiently. This opens an avenue for us to become greater than the angels."

Yusuf said "that is amazing, Grandpa! While fasting we are like angels and also have the opportunity to go beyond. Is that why fasting is an important act of worship?"

Grandpa nodded in affirmation to Yusuf's question. Both kids were very fascinated by this new knowledge they had gained and were curious to know more about fasting. Grandpa opened the Holy Quran in his hands and started reciting from Sura Baqara "O those who believe, fasting has been prescribed for you, as it was prescribed for those before you, so that you may become God conscious" (verse 183).

"One of the great effects of fasting is that it makes us conscious of Allah. Fasting instils the quality of taqwa in us." Grandpa turned towards Yusuf and asked him "When you were at school today and felt very thirsty, why didn't you drink water? No one was there to watch you neither your father nor mother or sister."

Yusuf was aware of Allah's Omniscience responded, "But Allah was watching me, we fast for Him and He would know if he secretly ate or drink something".

"Indeed, my child! A fasting person is not only careful of not eating or drinking but also not committing any sin because he sees himself infront of Allah and accountable to Him. If we keep reminding ourselves all throughout the Holy month of Ramzan that Allah is watching us, our soul would become conscious of being in His presence and this is the quality of Taqwa."

"Is taqwa the reward of fasting, Grandpa?", Jamila asked.

"Taqwa is one of the blessings of Allah bestowed upon believers who fast but the reward of fasting is much greater!", Grandpa said.

Yusuf who was gaining interest with every sentence in this conversation immediately added "We become like angels! That is the reward of fasting, isn't it Grandpa?"

"No, my dear child. Angelic traits are no doubt valuable, but Allah has set a higher reward for fasting?"

"What is that Grandpa?" both kids asked together.

"Allah says fasting is for me and I am His reward. A believer who fasts sincerely for Allah, Allah brings him closer to Himself, blesses that person with His love and opens the door of wisdom for him. Remember we learnt that soul and body are both closely connected to each other? When we give up permitted worldly pleasures for the sake of Allah's pleasure, he liberates our soul from the lowly desires. A liberated soul is capable of receiving divine favours and ascending towards His Lord." Grandpa explained to the kids.

"A liberated soul? What do you mean by a liberated soul, Grandpa" Yusuf innocently asked.

"Let me explain it to you in a different manner", said Grandpa. "When you are fasting, your mind is free from the worry of eating and drinking. You also engage more in acts of worship such as reciting Quran, duas and prayers. Your focus shifts from catering to the needs of your body to obedience of Allah which provides food for and strengthen your soul."

Jamila looking very serious now added "When our soul is strong, we can follow the desires of the soul better rather than the desires of body. That is what a liberated soul means."

Grandpa was very content with her granddaughter's understanding and smiled at her. "Indeed, my lovely daughter", he replied.

Excitement and awe were clearly showing on the faces of both kids after tis insightful conversation with their wise Grandpa. Suddenly, Yusuf jumped from the couch and ran from the living room. Seeing him so excited, Grandpa asked him "Where are you going, Yusuf?".

"I am going to tell the secret of fasting to Mother, Grandpa. I want to tell her that I will fast for the entire month of Ramzan to liberate my soul!"

Grandpa laughed at his innocent gesture and prayed to Allah in his heart to keep his children steadfast and accept their fasting in the blessed month of Ramzan.

# Animals in the Quran

## Prophet Musa (A) & The Sacrifice

**1**

A long time ago, there was a tribe known as the Banī Isrā'īl.* They were blessed to have a special Prophet of Allah in their tribe! Prophet Mūsā ('a)* helped the tribe and taught them about Allah. Still, some of them did not believe or follow Allah's rules.

There was one man in this tribe who was very rich. He had more gold, money, and jewels than he could even count!

On the other hand, the old man had two nephews who were very poor. They barely had enough to eat and drink! Instead of sharing his money with them, their uncle would spend all his time counting his treasures.

The rest of the tribe felt very sad seeing this. How could he treat his own family like this?! We should always share our blessings, especially with our family members.

**2**

One person in the tribe was so angry that he decided to kill the old man! This way, his poor nephews could have all his gold.

**3**

Early one morning, a traveler was passing through town when he stumbled across the dead body of the old man. Everyone began wondering, Who killed this man?! It wasn't long before everyone began accusing each other. The people wouldn't stop arguing! So, they finally decided to ask Prophet Mūsā ('a) for help. Of course, Prophet Mūsā ('a) knew exactly what to do! Al'amdulillāh!*

*Pronunciation Guide:
ḥ is a heavy "ha" sound that comes from the middle of the throat

**5**

## 4

Prophet Mūsā ('a) patiently listened to his tribe's problem.

After that, he announced, "I will pray to Allah and ask Him to show us who the killer is!"

Prophet Mūsā ('a) then went to a quiet place. With tears in his eyes, he prayed to Allah to show him how to fix this problem.

5

Allah answered Prophet Mūsā's ('a) du'ā. The solution was simple! All they had to do was sacrifice a cow. When the people heard this, they began laughing. They thought, How silly!

A cow is going to show us who the killer is?! Instead of trusting Allah and His Prophet, they started asking silly questions.

One man asked, "What kind of cow?"

Another asked, "Yeah, what color should it be?!"

Instead of getting angry at them for being disrespectful, Prophet Mūsā ('a) turned to Allah once again. And again, Allah answered each and every one of their silly questions.

When the tribe members heard Allah's specific answers, they looked at each other nervously. Making fun of Allah's Prophet had made their job so much harder! How were they going to find the exact cow Allah described?!

After searching far and wide, they finally found a cow that fit the description! It was a beautiful yellow cow at the far end of the city. Alhamdulillāh! But there was one slight problem. The little boy who owned this cow loved it very much. He didn't want to lose his favorite cow. The Banī Isrā'īl begged him. "We'll give you anything!" they offered.
"Anything?" asked the young boy. "Hmm, okay! I will sell you the cow if you pay me as much gold as she weighs!" (And cows weigh a lot!)
The tribe members glanced at each other anxiously. That was a lot of money! But they were so desperate to find the murderer that they had no other choice.

After everyone chipped in, they finally had enough money! What a shame! They had to pay so much money for this cow — only to sacrifice it! If only they had listened to Allah in the first place!

When they got back, Allah ordered Prophet Mūsā ('a) to rub the cow's tail against the body of the old man. Everyone watched in awe as Allah miraculously brought the man back to life! He lifted his head, pointed to one of his nephews, and shouted, "This is the boy who killed me!" Then, he lowered his head and died once more. Finally, the problem was solved!

The people quickly arrested the boy and put him in jail. They all learned a very important lesson from this experience! Allah asked them to complete a simple task: sacrifice a cow. However, instead of trusting Allah, they doubted Him and even made fun of His Prophet! This only made their simple job more difficult. Remember, we should always trust in Allah and listen to His Prophet. After all, He knows best!

# Battle of Ohad

*By Zahra Hasan*

Dear children, in the last issue we told you about the events of the first battle of Islam which was Badr. After the Battle of Badr, the infidels' lords and chiefs' confidence was badly shaken. They were thoroughly humiliated, so they were burning with the desire to take revenge from the Muslims. Soon they got busy in planning a second battle. They formed a large army and finalized the plans to attack Medina. Therefore, in 3 A.H their army charged towards Medina, and another battle emerged, which was later acknowledged as 'the battle of Ohad'.

Unlike last time, the Muslims managed to build a decent army. Altogether they were 1000 men and they had ample and good quality weapons, ready to fight for Islam. But here a new phenomenon arose, which was previously unknown to the Muslims. This was the coming forth of the munafiqeen (hypocrites) among the ranks of the Muslims community. Unexpectedly, on the eve of the battle, 300 people dragged themselves out of the Muslim army. They were led by a man with the name of Abdullah ibn Abi Salul. This sudden jolt apparently depleted the strength of the Muslims which is always the main motto of the munafiqeen.

The battle took place on 17th Shawwal 3 A.H, near the mountains of Ohad. There was a gorge or big hole on one side of the mountains, and it was feared that a group of the disbelieving army may sneakily attack from there. RasulAllah (pbuh) therefore assigned 50 archers to sit and stay on the mountain and guard the gorge. The archers were given very, very strict instructions to NOT leave their positions, no matter what happens. The leader of the kafir army was none other than Abu Sufyan, the father of Muawiya and the grandfather of Yazid.

One of the most predominant generals of the kafir army was Khalid bin Waleed, who was actually the one to think of the idea to execute a surprise attack on the Muslim army from that gorge! Soon after, the battle began, and the high faith and boosted morale of the Muslims caused the Kafir army to retreat and run away. It was a quick victory. But because of this swift victory, the Muslims got carried away. A bit too carried away. They dropped their weapons and began looting the remains (booty) of war. Even the archers ran from the mountain and wobbled down, eager to get their share (of the booty), while completely forgetting the strict orders of RasulAllah. The leader of the archers kept on yelling after them to come back, but his voice was drained down in the exclamations of excitement.

Only 3 archers were left on the mountain, including the leader. Remember Khalid bin Waleed's plan? Well, this was his golden opportunity and he and the small portion of the army came marching down. The 3 archers tried to block the attack but couldn't and they were soon martyred. The attack was very sudden and fell like a lightning bolt on all the Muslim soldiers who were busy collecting the booty. Not unexpectedly, they were caught off guard and were flabbergasted at the suddenness of the attack. Soon the scene reversed, and now the Muslims were the ones who were retreating.

Many Muslim soldiers were killed. Many others who tried to fight, including the uncle of RasulAllah Hazrat Ameer Hamza, were martyred. The contingent of Khalid bin Waleed was now on the march and their main target was RasulAllah, but they were blocked by some loyal companions and Imam Ali (pbuh).

There was mayhem everywhere. Some Muslims with weaker faith even began to think that RasulAllah was martyred, and they should switch sides and apologise to the kafir lords for accepting Islam. Imam Ali fought very bravely and broke multiple swords. It was in this battle that Imam Ali was given the legendary "Zulfiqar". There were a few companions that sacrificed their lives while protecting RasulAllah, including a woman. Eventually the attack of the kafireen was repulsed, but RasulAllah did get injured. He received wounds on his face and even broke a few teeth.

In all, 70 Muslims were martyred during the battle, including the amazing hero and beloved uncle of RasulAllah, Hazrat Ameer Hamza (he is also known as the first leader of martyrs or Sayid e Shohada). This testing scenario and the subsequent situation of Muslims is described by Allah in the holy Quran in the following two verses of Sura Aal e Imran (3). We are presenting the translation for a better understanding of what happened in the battle of Ohad:

"And surely Allah fulfilled His Promise when you easily conquered over them (the kafereen) by His permission, until you displayed weakness in courage and steadfastness, and you disputed and disobeyed (the command of RasulAllah) after you were shown what you loved (the war booty and wealth). Some among you are desirous of Dunya while some among you want Akherah. Then you were deprived of victory so that Allah may examine you and He (Allah) has pardoned you, and Allah is Gracious upon the momineen." (3:152)

"(Remember that on the day of Ohad) when you were running up the heights without even looking back and the Rasool was calling you from behind. Thus, He sent grief upon grief towards you (in response to your disobedience). (But now He expects you to) not grieve upon what is lost and the humility and injuries you suffered. Allah is All-Knowing about what you do." (3:153)

The battle of Ohad was a great lesson for the Muslims. They learnt that ignoring the orders and instructions of RasulAllah and getting greedy for the wealth of this Dunya can bring horrible consequences. It also brought to surface those Muslims that were disbelievers in their heart and who only acknowledged Islam by their deceitful tongues (Munafiqeen). This battle also made clear that Allah's help can only be acquired by complete obedience to RasulAllah and by being truthful to Islam.

# Kindness to Parents

And to your parents be good
Sūrah al-Isrā, Verse 23 (17:23)

﴿وَ بِالْوَالِدَيْنِ إِحْسَانًا﴾

Wa bil-wālidayni iḥsānā

Match each word or phrase with its correct definition!

| English | Arabic |
| --- | --- |
| Good | وَ |
| And | بِ |
| To | وَالِدَيْنِ |
| Parents | إِحْسَانًا |

# The grace of Allah

This is from the grace of my Lord
Sūrah an-Naml ,Verse 40 (27:40)

﴿هٰذَا مِنْ فَضْلِ رَبِّي﴾

Hādhā min faḍli Rabbī

Match each word or phrase with its correct definition!

| English | Arabic |
| --- | --- |
| From | هَذَا |
| My Lord | مِنْ |
| This | فَضْلِ |
| Grace | رَبِّي |

# Peace and Friendship

And (making) peace is better
Sūrah an-Nisā, Verse 128 (4:128)

﴿وَٱلصُّلْحُ خَيْرٌ﴾

Waṣ-ṣulḥu khayr

Match each word or phrase with its correct definition!

| English | Arabic |
| --- | --- |
| (Making) Peace | وَ |
| Better | اَلصُّلْحُ |
| And | خَيْرٌ |

# Praying for knowledge

My Lord! Increase my knowledge
Sūrah Tā Hā, Verse 114 (20:114)

﴿رَبِّ زِدْنِي عِلْماً﴾

Rabbi zidnī ʿilmā

Match each word or phrase with its correct definition!

| English | Arabic |
| --- | --- |
| Knowledge | رَبِّ |
| Increase my | زِدْنِي |
| My Lord | عِلْماً |

# Gratitude

*By Zahra Hasan*

From the burning sun to the glowing moon,

God has created all of this for me and you.

He created the animals that roam the earth,

And the sky that is big and blue.

We have seen Allah's signs and creations since birth, Including the trees and lovely birds.

He created us mankind with clay and mud,

We are so blessed that we can't even count what He has made word by word. When we see the creations of God like the flowers and the mighty ocean,

Then we should thank Him for what He has made with Alhamdulillah and gratitude.

# Nahjal Balaghah Series

## Sermon 155

### The Creation of a Bat

An example of Allah's delicate and wonderful creation which He has shown us can be seen in bats. Bats keep hidden in the daylight, although daylight reveals everything else, and move about in the night, although the night slows down every other living being. Their eyes get dazzled and cannot make use of the light of the sun to see things.

Allah has prevented bats from moving in the brightness of the sun and confined them to their places of hiding instead of going out at the time of its shining. Consequently, they keep their eyelids down in the day and treat night as a lamp, using it to search for their livelihood. The darkness of the night does not obstruct their sight nor does the gloom of darkness prevent them from movement. As soon as the sun rises and the rays of its light shine upon the lizards in their holes, the bats pull down their eyelids and live on what they had collected in the darkness of the night.

Glorified is He who has made the night as day for them to seek livelihood and made the day for their rest. He has given them wings of flesh with which they rise upwards to fly. They look like the ends of ears without feathers or bones. If you look closely, you can see the veins quite distinctly. They have two wings which are neither too thin to get bent during flying, nor too thick and heavy to lift. When they fly, their young ones hold on to them, getting down when they get down and rising up when they rise. The young ones do not leave until their limbs become strong and their wings can support them to rise, and when they begin to recognise their places of living and interests. Glorified is He who creates everything without any previous sample by someone else.

**Activity: Answer the questions below and fill in the blanks**
1. Do mommy bats fly with their young ones clinging to them? (True or False)?
2. When do the young ones leave their mothers?
3. Allah has prevented the bats from moving in the brightness of the _____.
4. Glorified is Allah who has made the night as day for them to seek _________ and made the day for _____.

**Activity for 15+ (Year 10 students)**

Bats are the only flying mammals. Paleontologists have found the oldest fossil of a bat dated to be over 52 million years old. According to scientists, the unexplained origin of this flying mammal is one of the greatest unsolved mysteries in evolution. Read the present theories on the evolution of bats. Write back to us and share your thoughts.

Ponder over the sermon: "Glorified is Allah who creates everything without any previous sample by someone else." See verse 49 of Surah Qamar (#54) in the Holy Quran.

# Hajj Cryptogram

Decode the message from the Quranic verses on pilgrimage. Each letter in the phrase has been replaced with a random number.

| A | B | C | D | E | F | G | H | I | J | K | L | M | N | O | P | Q | R | S | T | U | V | W | X | Y | Z |
|---|---|---|---|---|---|---|---|---|---|---|---|---|---|---|---|---|---|---|---|---|---|---|---|---|---|
|   |   |   |   |   |   |   | 19 | 26 |   |   |   | 20 |   |   | 3 |   |   |   |   |   |   |   |   |   |   |

I(26) _(9)  I(28) _(8)  _(22) _(10) _(11) _(5)  P(3) I(26) _(23) _(9) _(22)  _(9) H(19) _(24) _(9)  _(5) _(23) _(24) _(16) H(19) _(23) _(8)

H(19) I(26) M(20)

*Hint - 22:37*

| A | B | C | D | E | F | G | H | I | J | K | L | M | N | O | P | Q | R | S | T | U | V | W | X | Y | Z |
|---|---|---|---|---|---|---|---|---|---|---|---|---|---|---|---|---|---|---|---|---|---|---|---|---|---|
| 22 |   | 23 |   | 19 |   |   |   |   |   |   |   |   |   | 8 |   |   | 2 |   | 13 |   |   |   |   |   |   |

C(23) O(8) O(8) _(15) E(19) R(2) A(22) T(13) E(19)  _(6) _(26)  _(15) _(6) E(19) T(13) _(24)  A(22) _(26) _(5)

_(10) O(8) _(5) _(14) A(22) R(2) _(6) _(26) E(19) _(12) _(12)  _(1) _(20) T(13)  _(5) O(8)  _(26) O(8) T(13)

C(23) O(8) O(8) _(15) E(19) R(2) A(22) T(13) E(19)  _(6) _(26)  _(12) _(6) _(26)  A(22) _(26) _(5)

A(22) _(10) _(10) R(2) E(19) _(12) _(12) O(6) _(26)

*Hint - 5:2*

| A | B | C | D | E | F | G | H | I | J | K | L | M | N | O | P | Q | R | S | T | U | V | W | X | Y | Z |
|---|---|---|---|---|---|---|---|---|---|---|---|---|---|---|---|---|---|---|---|---|---|---|---|---|---|
| 10 |   | 12 |   | 19 | 9 |   |   |   |   |   | 4 | 21 |   | 8 |   |   |   |   | 1 |   |   |   |   |   |   |

T(1) E(16) _(19) _(15)  _(22) _(6) L(4) L(4)  C(12) _(7) M(21) E(19) T(1) _(7)  _(15) _(7) _(26)  _(7) _(20)  F(9) _(7) _(7) T(1)

A(10) _(20) _(13) _(7) _(20)  E(19) _(5) E(19) _(2) _(15)  L(4) E(19) A(10) _(20)  C(12) A(10) M(21) E(19) L(4)  _(1) T(16) E(19) _(15)

_(22) _(6) L(4) L(4)  C(12) _(7) M(21) E(19)  F(9) _(2) _(7) M(21)  E(19) _(5) E(19) _(2) _(15)  _(13) _(6) _(24)  T(1) A(10) _(20) T(1)

_(17) A(10) _(24) _(24)

*Hint — 22:27*

# Ancestors of Prophet Muhammad(S.A.W)

## Qusay and Abde Manaf

*By Samana Ali*

It was an ordinary day in the land of Syria, more than a century before the birth of Prophet Muhammad (peace be upon him). Fatima stood with a heavy heart as she waved goodbye to her dear son, Qusay, who was leaving his mother today to begin a new chapter of his life. Qusay had a very special place in his mother's heart, not only because he was her son but also because he was generous, brave, and sympathetic. His ideas were pure, and his manners were very refined. These virtues were the result of his belief in the One and only God, the Creator and Sustainer of the universe. Qusay, like all ancestors of the Holy Prophet throughout history, was a firm believer in Tawheed (monotheism) and followed the ways of Prophet Ibrahim (peace be upon him).

Although Qusay had happily lived with his mother Fatima and his stepfather Rabi'a in Syria for as long as he could remember, things had changed now. There were some differences between Rabia's tribe and Qusay. When Fatima saw that Qusay was not being treated fairly, she decided to send Qusay to his real father's family in Makkah. Yes, this was a goodbye with a heavy heart and Fatima would dearly miss her son, but she knew that this was the best decision for Qusay.

Qusay rode from Syria for days on end, mounted on his camel until he could see the mountains of Makkah as they stood tall, proud and mighty. Qusay felt a sense of belonging as if Makkah had always been his true home. After all, Makkah was not only Qusay's birthplace but also the city of the Ka'aba, the sacred house of Allah that Qusay's ancestors, Prophet Ibrahim and Prophet Ismail (peace be upon them) had built. In the next few days, Qusay realized that most people of Makkah had forgotten the Tawheed taught to them by Prophet Ibrahim and were involved in many vices such as drinking wine, gambling and even idol worshiping. They treated the weak with oppression and injustice. The practice of Hajj, however, was still carried out since the time of Prophet Ibrahim and Prophet Ismael, although it had become contaminated with idol worship. Although this was disappointing for Qusay, he was determined to serve Allah by helping the people of Makkah as well as the Pilgrims of His holy house, the Ka'ba, as best as he could.

Qusay realized that the well of Zamzam had been filled up long ago, but unfortunately, no one knew its original location. This made access to water very difficult for everyone, especially for the pilgrims who visited Ka'ba every year for Hajj. Qusay dug the first well in Makkah and established a supply of food and water to the pilgrims visiting the Ka'ba. Qusay knew that people coming to visit the Ka'ba were the guests of Allah. It gave him a lot of joy to serve them food and water, but he wanted to do more. After some efforts, he was able to make arrangements for the pilgrims to stay at Mash'arul-Haram at night (this is part of the Hajj rituals). Once more, showing his intelligence, he illuminated the valley with lamps, thus making their stay comfortable. Qusay established Dar-un-Nadwah (Assembly House) in Makkah. It was a place where discussions were held about important matters like war and peace. Caravans assembledbefore going out, and marriages and other ceremonies were conducted there. When Qusay became a young man, Hulail, the caretaker of the Ka'ba married his daughter to Qusay. When Hulail left the world, according to his will, Qusay became the caretaker of the Ka'ba. Because of his virtues and the services that Qusay had done for the people of Makkah and the pilgrims of the Ka'ba, he was considered an undisputed leader of the entire city.

Qusay had two sons, Abde Daar and Abde Manaf both of whom he loved dearly. As Abde Daar and Abde Manaf grew up, they followed the footsteps of their father and served the people of their city with true love and humility. At last, the day came when Qusay had to say goodbye to the world and meet the Lord whom he had served his whole life. This was a very heavy-hearted goodbye for his family and the people of Makkah, who both respected and loved Qusay. He was buried at Hajun (present-day Jannatul Mualla), and people from Makkah often visit his grave to pay their respects to their noble leader.

## The Moon of Bat'ha

Qusay had left the responsibility of taking care of the Kaaba and Darrun Nadwa as well as the pilgrims to Abde Daar before his death. However, as time passed it was realized that Abde Manaf was more capable than his brother. Regardless, Abde Manaf never became a rival for his brother and always assisted him with his responsibilities. Because of his wisdom, nobility and benevolence, Abde Manaf was considered the chief of the tribe of Quraish and people willingly obeyed him. Like his father, Adbe Manaf was a believer in Allah and was very generous, wise and virtuous. He cared for all people, especially his relatives. He was so dear to the people of Makkah that they called him the Moon of Bat'ha (Makkah).


Allah granted Abde Manaf 6 sons, of which Hashim and Abde Shams were twins. At birth, the two were stuck together with a piece of flesh, which was then separated with a sword. By some, it was considered a sign that there would be sword and bloodshed between these two brothers and their offspring for times to come. After Abde Daar and Abde Manaf died, things began to change between their families. There was a dispute between their sons as to who would carry the honor of being the caretaker of the Ka'ba, Darrun Nadwa and looking after the pilgrims. Both families wanted the honorable duties carried out by their grandfather Qusay, for themselves. Fortunately, they eventually decided to share responsibilities. The children of Abde Manaf were now settled in the Holy land of Makkah, and from amongst them rose great men of faith, virtue and honour who were to become the forefathers of the noblest of humans.

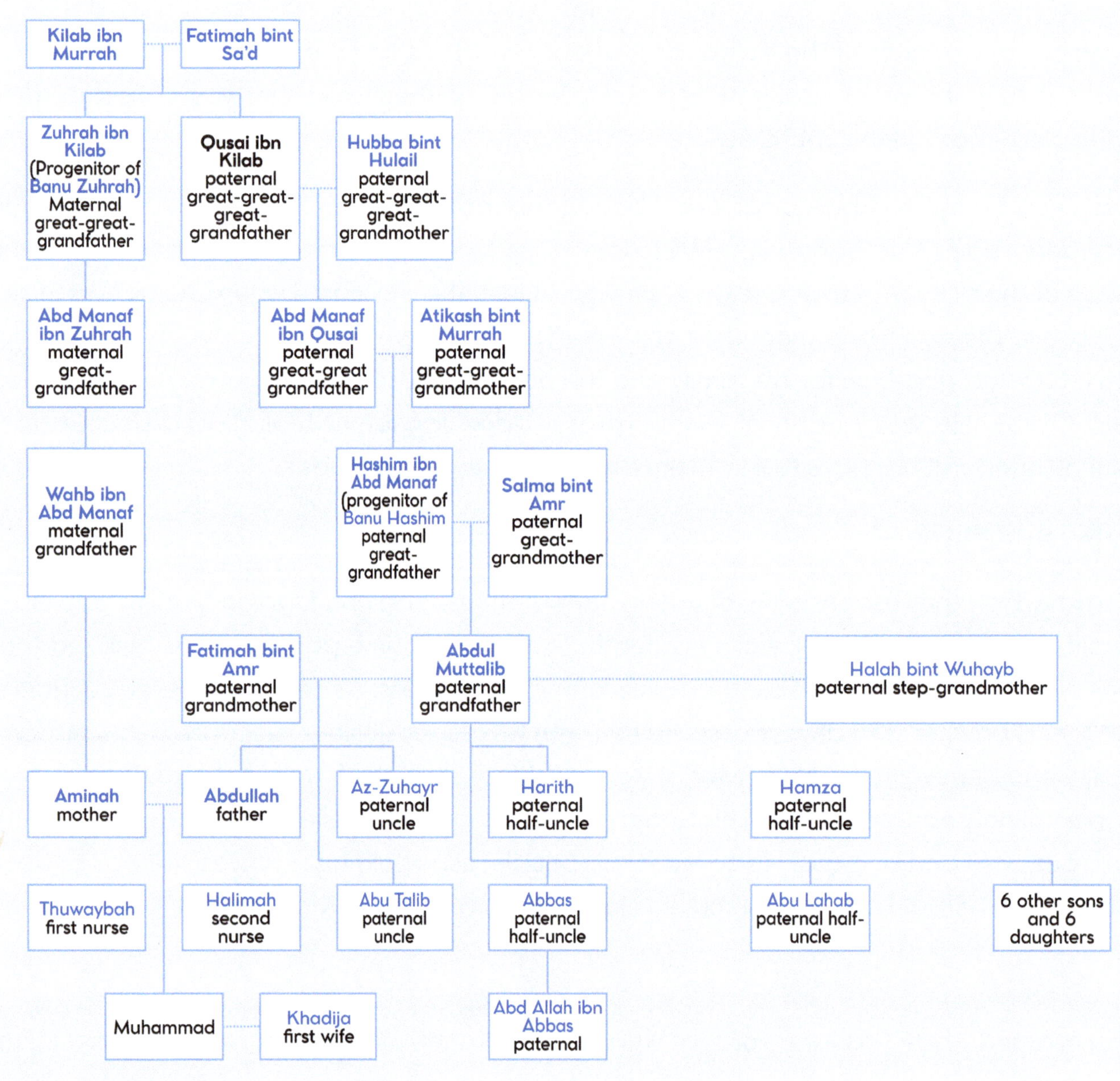

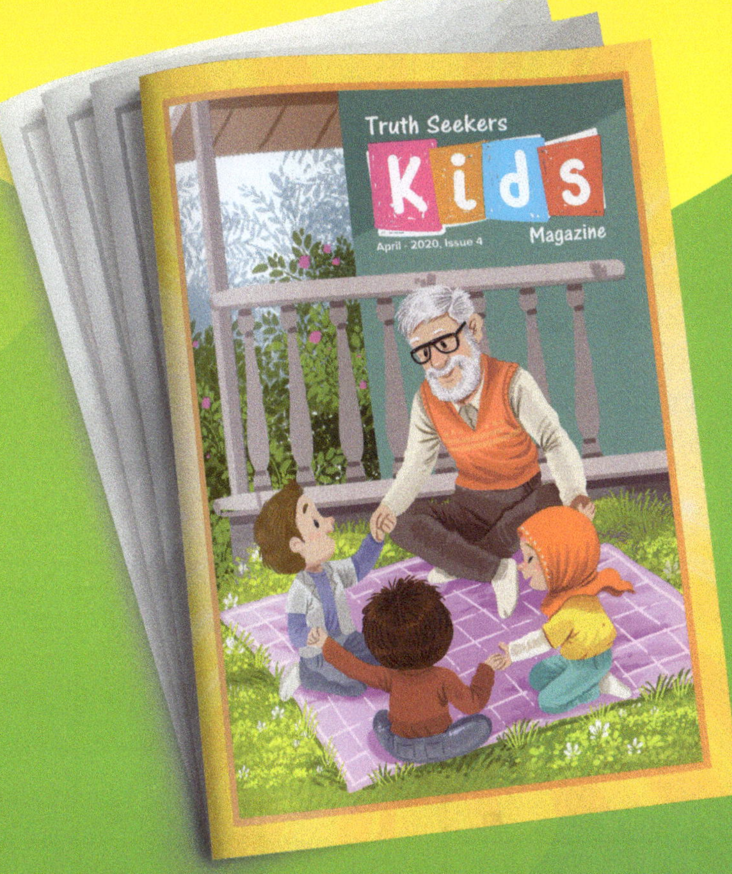


To subscribe,
scan this QR Code:

$35 AU
Every year

TS Kids Magazine - Subscription of 4 issues & free shipping

TS Kids Magazine hard copy 4 issues delivered in Australia
Free shipping | Digital version available on request

For subscription in other countries
Please contact us at:
magazine@tskids.club
For more info, visit us at:
www.tskids.club/plans-pricing

Please Follow and Like our Instagram and Facebook pages to get updates about TS Kids Magazine and much more.

 TSKidsClub     TSKidsClub

For more details, please visit **www.tskids.club/plans-pricing**

# Sura Al-Ma'un

## سورة الماعون

Surah Ma'un (Almsgiving) is the 107th surah of the Holy Quran and contains 7 verses. In this surah, Allah mentions those who deny the judgment, those who drive away the orphans, those who do not encourage feeding the poor, those who are not mindful of their prayers, those who make a show of their deeds and those who deny small acts of kindness.

Find the following words in the puzzle.

Words are in directions 

| | | | | | | | | | | | |
|---|---|---|---|---|---|---|---|---|---|---|---|
| س | غ | ج | ث | ز | ج | م | ي | ن | ا | ق | ه |
| ا | ث | د | ي | ن | ث | ظ | ت | ل | ى | ف | م |
| ه | ش | ق | د | س | ت | س | ي | ف | ا | ع | ص |
| و | ض | س | ض | ط | و | ح | م | ج | س | م | لّ |
| ن | ا | د | ث | خ | ع | ء | ن | ه | ر | ي | ي |
| ه | ر | ء | ا | ك | ة | ا | ث | و | ا | د | ن |
| ل | خ | س | ل | و | ر | ك | م | ى | ف | و | د |
| ك | ي | ي | ن | س | ك | م | ا | ع | و | ن | ح |
| م | س | ك | ي | ن | م | س | ن | ه | ت | ر | ة |
| ط | ن | و | ج | ا | ر | ل | غ | ص | ل | ا | ة |

**دين**

**طعام**

**مصلّين**

**ساهون**

**يتيم**

**مسكين**

**صلاة**

**ماعون**

# Little Contributors

By Tayyab Raza, age 11

By Fatima Hasan, age 8

By Mukhtar, age 5

By Zainab Zahra Hussain, age 7

**SUBMIT YOUR WORK**

Hey kids! Would you like to submit your poem, writing or drawing?

Send it to us by email at **magazine@tskids.club**

# Arabictivity

## Learn words from the Quran by tracing the word in Arabic

| | | | |
|---|---|---|---|
| الدين | الدين | الدين | الدين |
| الطعام | الطعام | الطعام | الطعام |
| المصلّين | المصلّين | المصلّين | المصلّين |
| الساهون | الساهون | الساهون | الساهون |
| اليتيم | اليتيم | اليتيم | اليتيم |
| المسكين | المسكين | المسكين | المسكين |
| الصلاة | الصلاة | الصلاة | الصلاة |
| الماعون | الماعون | الماعون | الماعون |

# Mathematica

## Race to the number 14

This game of addition can be played between two players, A and B.

Player A should choose and tell any number from 1 to 3.

Player B should choose any number from 1 to 3 and add it to player A's number.

Player A should choose any number from 1 to 3 and add to player B's number.

Both players should keep taking turns until the numbers reach 14.

The player who adds the last number to reach 14 is the winner.

For example,

i. player A chooses 2
ii. player B chooses 3: 2+3 = 5
iii. player A chooses 3: 5+3 = 8
iv. player B chooses 3: 8+3 = 11
v. player A choose 3: 11+3 = 14
vi. Winner is player A

---

## Imam Ali's Mathematical Brilliance

### Dividing 17 Camels

A person was about to die, and before dying he wrote his will which went as follows: "I have 17 camels, and I have three sons. Divide my camels in such a way that my eldest son gets half of them, the second one gets 1/3rd of the total and my youngest son gets 1/9th of the total number of camels."

After his death when the relatives read his will, they got extremely perplexed and wondered how they could divide 17 camels this way.

After a long, hard thought they decided that there was only one man in Arabia who could help them - Imam Ali (peace be upon him).

So they all came to the door of Imam Ali and put forward their problem.

Imam Ali said, "Ok, I will divide the camels as per the man's will."

Imam Ali said, "I will lend one of my camels to the total which makes it 18 (17+1=18), now let's divide as per his will."

The eldest son gets       1/2 of 18 = 9
The second one gets     1/3 of 18 = 6
The youngest gets        1/9 of 18 = 2
Now the total number of camels  = 17 (9+6+2=17)
Then Imam Ali said, "Now I will take my camel back."

In this series, we will meet real life superheroes who have made significant achievements and contributions to our society and community, as well as in their fields of discipline. In this issue, we take inspiration from Emeritus Professor Syed Hasan Masood.

Born to a mathematician and a school principal in a modest city of India, this young boy with innocence in his eyes, honesty in his demeanor, and hope in his heart was meant to make a difference in the world.

Professor Masood was raised in Lucknow, India (a city with a rich Shia heritage, and famous for preserving centuries of Azadari traditions). After his schooling in Lucknow, he went to study Engineering at one of the premier institutes - Aligarh Muslim University in India.

With higher education not so popular among the Muslims in the 1970s and 80s, Prof. Masoof received a full

scholarship for Masters in Engineering at the University of New Brunswick in Canada. He also completed a postgraduate diploma from IIT Delhi, India. Not stopping there and with his thirst for knowledge, Prof. Masood again became a recipient for a full PhD scholarship where he finally moved down under at the University of Queensland. Soon after his PhD, he became a lecturer (later promoted to professor) at the Department of Manufacturing Engineering, Swinburne University, Australia in 1988.

## His Legacy

With his sincerity, hard work and the blessings of Allah, he received numerous accolades for his contributions of over 30 years in teaching and research especially in areas of additive manufacturing processes such as fused deposition modeling, selective laser melting or direct metal deposition (popularly known as 3D printing). The applications of his scientific research have been translated to products in the field of robotics, transportation and biomedical implants, as well as plastics and metals used in several industries. Prof. Masood has produced more than 400 publications in the form of research papers, books and book chapters. He has alsosupervised 27 PhD students and 13 Masters students, and more than 200 Masters by coursework students.

One of his tremendous feats lies in securing 23 competitive grants from the Australian Research Council, worth more than $10 million. In addition to the quantitative accomplishments, he has inspired numeorus students and peers for which he received a Lifetime Achievement Award at Swinburne University. Recently (2022), he was further awarded the title of Emeritus Professor for his outstanding contributions to the field of Advanced Manufacturing Technology at Swinburne University.

Vice Chancellor and President of Swinburne University, Professor Pascale Quester has said, "Prof. Masood's legacy at Swinburne lives through the success of his students". This indeed is true as many of his students have become academics, business leaders and expert engineers.

## His service to Islam

With a very modest, gentle and committed personality, Prof. Masood has dedicated his life to the service of Islam. Without revealing much details of his numerous noble acts, he has greatly contributed towards establishing the first Shia Islamic center in Melbourne, teaching jurisprudence in an Islamic Sunday school, inspiring others to abide by Islamic law and ethics, helping families in various ways and leading from the front for any noble cause.

Those who know Prof. Masood personally would unanimously agree that he has truly inspired the lives of so many around him, whether they be migrants to Australia or people across the world. Although he has been a superhero in many ways, the thing that stands out the most is his unwavering dedication in striving to please Allah alone. Both through his words and actions he has encouraged all others to do so too, and use all our blessings as the means towards Him.

Prof. Masood's life after retirement is spent with his wife, children and grandchildren, as well as his close family members, friends and members of the community.

We are excited to launch the

## Truth Seekers Foundation
# Members Hub.

### What is TSF Members Hub?

TSF Members Hub is an exclusive members area which contains several exciting products from Truth Seekers Foundation.

These include

- Our newly launched TS Illumination Magazine
- TS Kids Magazine
- Exclusive books published by TSF and its partners
- Regular digital and media content
- Discussion forum exclusive for members
- A platform to get involved with our charity projects
- Monthly newsletters

All of these can be accessed from the members area at

 **members.truthseekersfoundation.org**

or via scanning the QR code

---

To become a member, you are required to sign up, create a profile and register for the TSF Members Plan.

The fee to become a regular TSF member is just AUD 20 per month.

Please contact us if you have any queries regarding membership.